T0149440

FOOD for THOUGHT

A Life-changing Perspective

Arletha Simpson

FOOD FOR THOUGHT
A LIFE-CHANGING PERSPECTIVE

iUniverse books may be ordered through booksellers or by contacting:

iUniverse
1663 Liberty Drive
Bloomington, IN 47403
www.iuniverse.com
1-800-Authors (1-800-288-4677)

Because of the dynamic nature of the Internet, any web addresses or links contained in this book may have changed since publication and may no longer be valid. The views expressed in this work are solely those of the author and do not necessarily reflect the views of the publisher, and the publisher hereby disclaims any responsibility for them.

Any people depicted in stock imagery provided by Thinkstock are models, and such images are being used for illustrative purposes only. Certain stock imagery © Thinkstock.

ISBN: 978-1-4917-2310-4 (sc)
ISBN: 978-1-4917-2311-1 (e)

Library of Congress Control Number: 2014901375

Print information available on the last page.

iUniverse rev. date: 05/18/2015

Contents

Acknowledgments

(Forever Thankful)

Let me begin by recognizing the one reason I am who I am—Jesus Christ and his unconditional love and grace. To my daughter, Kristie: I can never thank you enough for all the sacrifices you've made to support and encourage me while writing this book. Thank you for being in my life.

Introduction

Life change teaches values and helps you to grow and transform your life. A life change can alter the circumstances of life. Change affects your actions and decisions—everything that you do on a daily basis for good or bad. So often, you are caught up by urgent things in life. Your material responsibility and day-to-day struggles create a vicious circle of fears, doubts, anxieties, and worries.

Whatever your particular need, you can find help in this book. The variety of topics—from "Actions" to "Wisdom"—are arranged alphabetically for easy use.

Actions

When you want someone to behave in a certain way, you must behave that way yourself. Then you will earn the right to be heard.

Our words lack significance if our actions don't back them up.

Foolish people often find it difficult to avoid trouble.

Don't let desire for praise, fame, and acceptance drive you to Sin.

It's not so much the events or circumstances that matter in life as it is your response to those events or circumstance.

Salvation does not depend on good deeds; it results in good deeds.

Don't let your reaction to having faith keep you from the healing you need the most.

You may think it's all right to be close to sin as long as you don't take part in it. "After all," you may say, "I won't do anything wrong." But being close to sin can hurt you, as you become attracted to sin and finally give in. The only sure way to stay away from sin is to *stay away*.

Truly admitting your mistakes is a step closer to solving them.

A smart man gets a lot of advice; a wise man evaluates the advice he gets.

Becoming absorbed in particulars makes us forget the principal cause for our actions.

Mistakes are not as significant as what can be learned from them.

Don't blame others for the choices you make take the responsibility for your own actions.

Guilt over certain actions can last a lifetime.

Doing what is right may be a costly commitment but a worthwhile one.

Don't throw away the instructions of the Bible because you think certain details are insignificant or unimportant.

When you don't do the job right the first time, it often becomes much more difficult to accomplish.

If you set out to use individuals, you will find yourself being used.

Putting off doing something often makes the situation worse.

Don't fault others for your mistakes.

A bad solution is worse than no solution.

Beliefs

The magnitude in the way you conduct yourself speaks volume about what you believe.

Your spiritual maturity goes above what you believe; it becomes a dynamic part of all you do, resulting in good fruit.

When you become so much like the world, no one can tell who you are or what you believe.

Don't form a negative opinion or conclusion about others in order to build yourself up.

No matter what you do, you cannot be separated from what you believe.

Don't allow another person to dictate your beliefs or actions.

Regardless of what you say outwardly, your actions will line up accordingly with your beliefs.

The information to which you give credibility often becomes what you believe.

If you know something but do not believe in it, that knowledge will not change your life.

If you believe in something, you are empowered to act differently.

Change

If you live like the world, then the world has no reason to change.

Changing locations won't change God's will. Learn to face the root of your problems. Moving away to escape problems only makes solving them more difficult. Problems rooted in you are not solved by a change of scenery or a change in location. This only pulls you away from the need to change your heart.

Toss away your old way of living, and move ahead into your new life of change.

God transforms those who seem unreachable. God is not slack concerning his promise, but is longsuffering toward us, not willing that any should perish but all come to repentance.

God is our foundation in the midst of change.

A changed life is the result of true remorse.

You may work hard to keep your outward appearance attractive, but what's in your heart is even more important. Deep down, where others can't see, matters to God.

Change comes when your old ways and attitudes are replaced by new ones.

To live differently, you must think differently.

Don't give up hope on yourself or others. Remember that God can work a complete change in you.

A changed mind and a changed heart bring forth a changed life.

You cannot change your life until God changes your heart.

Character

Your way of living and your connections to others provide a window into your personality.

The true worth of a person is solely in God created in His image gives us a solid basis for self-worth.

Your personality is often made known by how you respond to the unexpected.

Family character can influence children in the direction of good or evil.

Sometimes doing what's right or good will not always make you popular.

Don't pretend to be something you're not. Be who God intended you to be.

Better to question out loud than to doubt in silence.

Kind words can make a difference in a person's life.

The words you leave behind will be a permanent image of who you are.

Integrity is shown by how hard you work when no one is looking.

When you are tested through difficult circumstances, you can complain, or you can try to see how God is stretching you to develop your character.

Doing wrong can bring hurt and disappointment and degrade your character.

Appearances don't reveal what people are really like or what their true value is.

The depth of your character is revealed by how you react under pressure.

Instead of complaining about your struggles, see them as opportunities for growth.

Doubt

If you never struggle, your faith will never grow.

When you doubt, it can leave you as unstable as the restless waves. In order to stop being tossed about, lean on God and trust that he will show you what is best for you.

Even if our hearts convict us, God is larger than our hearts. His forgiveness and cleansing are enough; they override our doubts.

When distrust becomes stubbornness, and stubbornness becomes a way of life, don't stop there. Let your doubt deepen your faith as you continue to search for God.

Doubt leads to questions, questions lead to answers, and the answers are accepted. Then doubt has done good work.

If you are afraid when troubles surround you, it's because you doubt his ability to help.

If circumstances have turned against you, don't blame God; seek him.

When you feel worried or frightened that you cannot think or behave calmly, confess your need, and then trust God to care for you.

When life goes against you, it is tempting to think that God also is against you. The opposite is true; he is with you.

Just as an athlete needs continual practices to perfect his game, you also need constant reminders of the foundation of your faith and belief.

Faith

Highly trained and skilled athletes lose their power or capacity to perform if their muscles are not toned by continual use. You also can lose your spiritual talents if you don't put them to use.

If there is no persecution, it is hard to share your faith in God.

Don't be disappointed when people don't understand you, find fault in you, judge you, or even try to hurt you because of what you believe and how you live.

Never give up. Keep on living as you know you should. Jesus is the only One you need to please.

No matter how hard the fight, keep fighting.

Frame your faith on the foundation of a truthful God who never lies. He's the source of all truth. He cannot lie.

If God is slow in answering your prayers, just remember he might be testing your faith.

Being without faith keeps people from the truth and deprives them of hope.

Achievement is not measured by the quantity of what you have but your faith in God.

Do not lose your eternal blessings for temporary benefits.

Insults can hurt your emotions, but never let that change your faith.

A building is only as solid as its foundation.

Don't be satisfied with having the right answers about Jesus. Let your life show that the power of Jesus is working in you.

People judge others by outward appearances, often dismissing individuals who lack the particular physical qualities that society admires. Appearances, however, don't reveal what people are really like or what their true value is. Fortunately, God judges by faith and character, not appearances.

When God tests your faith, don't complain; just know he may be stretching you to develop your character.

Without faith to understand what God has done you, you remain unchanged.

Money is useless. No matter how much wealth you accumulate in this life, it will be of no use when you stand before your Creator. It will be your faith that saves you, not your bank accounts.

Do not become so preoccupied with your own faith that you neglect to share it with those around you.

When you face difficulties and your resources are low, and your doubts are the strongest, remember that God can open the floodgates of heaven.

God gives you the power to overcome your obstacles, but when you are filled with fear and doubt, you let difficulties rule your life. Regardless of your situation, you can have courageous, overcoming faith.

Faith is dominated by what is real and right.

God answers to faith, even in the middle of failure.

The true quality of a Christian is not revealed by the way he or she acts but by the way he or she reacts to life's adversities.

When facing persecution and your faith is bending under pressure. Fix your eyes on Jesus, who volunteered to die on your behalf.

You may not always see the effects of your faith, but you can be sure that God will honor faithfulness.

Faith is not stored away like money in the bank. Growing in faith is a constant process of daily renewing your trust in God.

You cannot have everything you pray for, as if by magic, but with faith, you can have everything you need.

God does not guarantee a life of comfort and ease. It is tough faith; a constant commitment to hang on and believe God against all odds, no matter what.

Keep your eyes on the prize, despite nagging temptations that tries to stop you, refuse to let up until you cross the finish line.

Fear

Get over your anxiety or concern of what people might say or do. Take your eyes off people and look to God.

Don't allow people to put fear in you. This neutralizes your effectiveness for the kingdom.

Planning for the future is time well spent; being anxious about tomorrow is time wasted.

Take courageous action in the presence of fear.

You may be hesitant to clear out all the wicked people in your life because you are afraid, because they seem harmless, or because you don't want to let go of a bad habit, an unhealthy relationship, or a certain lifestyle. You can allow these things to control you, but they will cause you serious problems later.

Fear of failure may make you afraid to do anything that might draw criticism or give someone a chance to laugh at you, but you can do everything through God, who gives us strength.

Satan is a master at using our fears to stop us, to bind us, and to rob us from serving God, but God has not given us the spirit of fear but power and a sound mind.

Whenever you start to fear, stop and pray.

Whenever you start to worry or feel anxious about life, turn your worries into prayers.

Let God's peace guard your heart against anxiety.

You may be confused by the events around you and so many things you'll never understand, so you worry and fear the unknown because you don't understand everything as it happens. Instead, you should trust that God knows what he's doing, even if his timing or design is not clear to you.

There is no fear in love. Perfect love drives out fear.

You may worry about details over which you have no control, while neglecting specific areas, such as attitudes, relationships, and responsibilities that *are* under your control. Concentrate on what God has given you to do, and leave the rest to God.

Do not conform to the pattern of this life, but change your mind-set.

When you think biblically, you have a sound mind. When you have a sound mind, fear just doesn't make sense.

Conquering fear is not a matter of self-determination; it is a matter of dependence on the God you can trust and love.

New situations or surroundings can frighten you. Recognize that experiencing fear is normal, but becoming paralyzed by fear is indication that you question God's ability to take care of you.

Follow God out of love rather than fear.

Forgiveness

Asking for forgiveness is essential, in spite of your pain.

A forgiving heart is necessary in order for your heart to heal.

Holding on to unforgiveness will destroy you spiritually and destroy your physical well-being.

Unforgiveness will take you to your grave. Let go of anger, hatred, grudges, and the people who have caused you so much pain. When you don't forgive, they still have power over you. Take your power back by forgiving. Then you can heal and have the peace within that only God gives, so you can move on with your life.

If you lose sight of the seriousness of sin, you'll lose the excitement of knowing you're forgiven.

It's never too late to put away bitterness and forgive.

Forgive and forget. Don't allow the past to keep you from your future. God forgives your sin. He separates it from you and doesn't remember it anymore.

Forgiveness is confined within certain limits. It's not limited by the amount of guilt you have but by your readiness to repent.

If you struggle with unforgiveness, it may be because you can't forgive yourself for something you've done.

Don't allow problem relationships to go unresolved.

When you imagine the worst, you give God no credit for the truth that he can heal your wounds and fix your problems.

You may live in fear every day because of your past hurts.

Forgive those who have wronged you.

Forgiving others is very hard, but it's necessary. Break out from the bondage of unforgiveness.

Unforgiveness can prevent you from receiving God's forgiveness. It puts up a wall between you and the source of your healing.

Let go and let God. Don't let what a friend, family, neighbor, boss, or coworker has done continue to bring you under bondage. Let that poison out of your heart. Let God heal the wound others have caused.

Don't let another day go by without taking care of the issues you have with another.

Two things that paralyze are the unwillingness to ask forgiveness and the bitter spirit that won't grant it to someone else.

Allowing yourself to hang on to hard feelings and become bitter only causes your wound to become more infected spiritually.

Forgiveness is a choice. Let God handle those who have wronged you. Put it in his hands and leave it there.

Forgive, for it takes the love and power of God working within you to make forgiveness possible.

It is easy to ask for forgiveness but difficult to grant it to others.

God

Whatever defeat, setbacks, or doubt you face, you can trust God totally, no matter what it is.

God will never turn his back on you, even when you turn your back on him.

You cannot uphold the teachings of scripture to match your beliefs. If you do, you put yourself higher than God.

Someone facing a life-or-death situation can be comforted by knowing that God will bring you safely through death to his kingdom.

Trust God with your life, even when life makes no sense.

What seems unchangeable, God can change and transform, giving new direction and meaning.

You can spend a lifetime accumulating human wisdom, yet never learn to have a personal relationship with God.

Never get so tired of doing right that you quit on God.

Just as plants draw nourishment from the soil through their roots, you also draw your life—giving strength from God.

God knows what you think and sees what you do.

Don't limit God by your expectations.

When you read rule books, the authors never come to help you follow the rules, but God does.

Be open to honest criticism. God may be speaking to you through others.

You may be arrogant enough to think you don't need God, but your every breath depends on the spirit he has breathed into you.

Wealth, more than need, can weaken your spiritual vision, because it tends to make you self-sufficient and eager to acquire still more of everything—except God.

When you have more than enough in abundance, you may take credit for your riches and become proud that your own hard work and intelligence has made you rich. You may push God right out of your life, but God gives you everything you have, and he asks you to manage it for him.

God looks at your troubles and issues in a different way than you do because God is eternal, he sees the past, present and the future all at the same time. He sees the end from the beginning. If we learn to look at life and people through God's eyes, everything changes.

Being satisfied with what you are or what you have comes from God.

Life is God's breath that you breathe.

Sometimes God gives instructions that do not seem appropriate to you at that moment.

Don't try to obey God by carefully choosing which commands you will obey and which you will ignore.

Worldly security is unsure, but God security is sure.

The word is your highest standard of service for testing everything else that claims to be true. It is your protection against false teaching and your model of guidance for how you should live.

You may want God's feast before you are spiritually capable of digesting it.

Your background does not matter to God; your background does not keep God from working in your life.

God plans are not dictated by human-actions or deeds.

Hope

Sometimes in life, your circumstances look hopeless, but remember that God can do the impossible.

Being without faith keeps you from the truth and rob you of hope.

Experiencing life difficulties help you to grow and give you hope for the future.

When the shadows of life get dark and heavy, know that somewhere on the other side of all these troubles is a ray of hope.

God is our bridge over troubled waters.

When we go through failure and disappointments, God covers us with victory.

When we fall, God picks us up. And every time we get knocked down, he tells us to get back up again.

We can live a happy and blessed life, even when troubles come our way.

Trials are inevitable. We can't go around them, over them, or under them; we must go through them.

When life throws you curveballs, don't look back; just look up.

God uses life's challenges and the devil attacks to build character.

When going through hard times, remember that for every problem you have, God is the problem solver.

God is the answer to your hope, no matter what you are going through.

Don't ever give up hope; God has a wonderful future in store for you.

Life

The pathway to life is slim, and the road is small; only a few find it.

The true test in life is how you handle everyday situations.

Living in a fast-paced world, there always seems to be something to do and no time for relaxation.

Life is short, no matter how long you live.

It's never easy to suffer pain. It's a part of life, no matter what the cause.

Life is full of little treasures that you take for granted every day our family, children, friends, spouses, wives, co-workers don't assume anything not appreciating people for what they are in your life. Showing your love and gratitude because life is short.

Separated from Jesus, life is brief and empty.

You make life's journey more difficult than necessary by lack of obedience.

Living is more than just stretching out; it requires work.

When trying to find familiar ground with those to whom you witness, be careful not to fall into the bed of compromise.

Sometimes you may become distracted with problems when you should be looking for opportunities. Instead of focusing on the negatives, develop an attitude of expectancy.

The state of being free doesn't come until you no longer have to prove your freedom.

Effectual living is not measured by what you achieve but by what you overcome to achieve it.

Pain is not always punishment but to humble you to trust that God would make you strong in weakness to glorify Him through our struggles.

Endurance often brings recognition to the one who endures to the end.

Freedom does not rest in possessions or things but in the One who gave you the freedom.

Being a Christian doesn't guarantee a trouble-free life.

Love

True service is motivated by love and devotion and seeks no personal gain.

A gentle, loving person gives light to the face that cannot be duplicated by the best cosmetic surgeon in the world.

Expressing appreciation, kindness, and gratitude should be the life of every believer.

It's easy to be kind to others when everything is going well. Are you still kind when others treat you unfairly?

Go slow when giving advice or counsel to those who are hurting. People often need compassion more than they need guidance.

True love is an action, not a feeling.

When you have been through hurt and pain, you are able to reach out with compassion to others who hurt.

It's not hard to refrain from hurting others, but it's much more difficult to take the initiative to do something good for someone.

If you truly love God and your neighbor, you will naturally keep the Commandments, rather than worrying about all you should not do. Concentrate on all you can do to show your love for God.

Genuine godlike love knows no boundaries, sets no limits, and draws no lines.

Love is not an option. Anything minus love equals nothing.

Love loves, even when it hurts.

True love freely opens its hands and gives away everything He has for us.

Loving God and loving your neighbor cannot be separated.

True love is love without limits. If you really love someone, no sacrifice is too great.

When you are uncertain about what to do, ask yourself which course of action best demonstrates love for God and love for others.

Let love rule your thoughts, decisions, and actions.

Mind-Set

What you choose to fill your mind will make a difference in the way you think and act.

A mind filled with good intentions has no room for evil thoughts.

When you're not thinking about your life's purpose, you are headed for self-destruction.

Many decisions cannot be changed. Think of the consequences before you launch into something you may later regret.

In tough situations, are you usually concerned first about yourself? Or do you consider the person most likely affected by the problem and find the solution for it?

It's possible to work hard and still lose everything if the decision is wrong or the means to carry it out are not in place.

Bad judgments are made when people don't think clearly.

To move and possess new life, you must drive out evil thoughts and practices.

What you put in your mind determines what comes out in your words and actions.

Evaluating yourself by man's standards of success and achievement can cause you to think too much about your worth in the eyes of others and thus, you'll miss your true value in God's eyes.

Careless decisions often lead to failure in gaining what is most valuable.

Healthy self-esteem is important. Some people think too little of themselves, or they may overestimate themselves. The key to honest and accurate evaluation is in knowing the basis of your self-worth. You are valuable and capable of worthiness in Christ.

Change your thoughts to change your actions.

How you view things in life—from the economy, to religion, to practical living—can affect your destiny. The choices you make today will affect your tomorrow.

Prayer

Prayer is necessary to conquer the desire of temptation.

The first step in any adventure is to pray.

Prayer is not always about you and yours but the needs of others.

When you are bruised and broken by the pressures of life, consider prayer.

Don't look for solutions to life's problems in the natural world; seek God, who has the answer for solving your problems.

You may have a busy schedule and always be in a hurry, flooded with many responsibilities, but there comes a time in your day when you ought to slow down and pray.

Prayer doesn't prepare you for battle, but the battle prepares you when you pray. Your best prayers are in your brokenness.

If there is no effort given to prayer, things often end in failure. When you pray effectively, you will see great results.

When you don't pray, it seems that you can do little, but after you have prayed, it seems as if you can do anything.

Prayer is the ladder of many horizons. To get to the top, you must start at the bottom and steadily rise upward.

Make a determined effort to pray when you feel like complaining, because complaining only raises your level of stress.

Prayer is when you reach into the deepest part of yourself and admit your needs and failures.

Prayer can change you, because in prayer, you are in the presence of God.

Prayer is the key that unlocks faith in your life.

There is no substitute for prayer, especially in circumstances that seem impossible.

The assurance of answered prayer brings peace.

Effective prayer needs an attitude, complete dependence, and an action—asking.

Pride

Unfulfilled and self-satisfied people are an easy mark for the devil.

Selfishness is not wrong within itself. It depends on what makes you selfish and what you do with your selfishness.

Pride can make you self-centered and lead you to believe that you deserve all you can see, touch, or imagine. It creates greedy appetites.

Don't admire people who look out only for themselves.

You may strike out at innocent people who get in your way, because you are ashamed or embarrassed because your pride is hurt. Lashing out at others can be a sign that something is wrong with you. Don't allow your own hurt or pride to lead you to hurt others.

Pride points to your own accomplishments, rather than to God. It is an attitude that elevates your effort or abilities above him, and it causes you to congratulate yourself for your successes and to look down on other people.

Pride and insecurity can cause you to overestimate your position and status.

Your heart's devotion can sometimes sway to and fro by thoughts of prideful temptation, but run to the One who can help and give you understanding.

Sometimes you take little account of your weaknesses and do not anticipate the stumbling blocks.

Independence promotes self-sufficiency, rather than God-sufficiency.

Pride arises from trying to do more than God intends, instead of letting him order our day.

Pride is one of the devil's methods of operation and weapons of warfare. It tempts you to take your eyes off God and places them on yourself.

You may not admit your failures. Instead, you continue to push forward, seeking self-gratification.

The enemy set traps for your life. If you are not careful or discerning, you will fall victim as one helpless or unable to resist attack.

Pride moves in a quiet, clever way. It shows no mercy and rarely announces its coming.

Purpose

When you don't have a proper foundation, you likely will quit during hard times.

Your inadequacies and lack of ability should not keep you from being effective for God.

Perseverance does not come naturally to some; it's a result of strong character.

When you try to measure up to society's standards for fame and success, you neglect your true purpose.

Withholding the truth leaves you without purpose and direction.

Following God's guidance, you know that you are where Christ wants you, whether you're moving or staying in one place.

Your spiritual journey may be lengthy, and you may face pain, discouragement, and difficulties, but remember: God isn't just trying to keep you alive. He wants to prepare you to live in service and devotion to him.

In your zeal for the truth of scripture, you must never forget its purpose is to equip you to do well.

Always live a life in such a way that you have a good answer, not for others but for yourself.

There is a relationship that makes life complete. Without that relationship, there is a void in life.

When you feel discouraged or inadequate, remember that God has always thought of you as valuable and that he has a purpose in mind for you.

To make the most of life, include God's plan in your plans.

Responsibility

Victimizing or finding fault with others is easier than owning up to your own shortcomings.

Stop making excuses, and take accountability for the choices you make.

Cleansing your hands of hard situations doesn't nullify your guilt; it only gives a false sense of peace.

Accepting responsibility is difficult, but it builds character and confidence, and it will earn you respect from others. It motivates you to do what Christ has called you to do, and it commits you to seeing it through.

No plan is complete until each job is assigned and everyone understands his or her responsibility.

Rather than trying to handle larger responsibilities alone, look for ways of sharing the load so that others may exercise their God-given gifts and abilities.

Everyone's life requires certain duties that present big demands.

Making an effort to excel in small tasks prepares you for greater responsibilities.

If you accept a responsibility, you must carry it out with determination and courage, regardless of the personal sacrifice.

If you don't take responsibility for what happens in your life, you're allowing others to decide your life for you.

Success

You may enjoy impressing people with your skills, but a high position based on deceit is nothing.

A lesson learned is an entrance to promotion and success.

Always be on guard for those people who try to convince you that how you live is more important than what you believe.

Always guard against favoritism; don't give priority to some and ignore others.

Be on the lookout for those who put more emphasis on their own success than on God's kingdom.

There is no accomplishment without risk of failing, no recognition without hard work, and no opportunity without criticism.

An effective person not only learns from his master, but also builds upon his master's achievements.

You will find true wealth by developing your spiritual life, not by developing financial assets. God is interested in what is lasting, not in what is temporary.

God does not measure success by what you possess but by your success in changing your life.

Temptation

Temptation has consequences. No one gets away without consequence forever. One day, your actions will be known to everyone.

In life's travels, you may build centers of false worship in your life—anything that causes you to turn your heart from God and do wrong. Never revel in false praise and compliments to further your own interests by thinking you're too strong to be tempted.

No sin is a little sin. Each one carries the same consequences.

Run from anything you know is wrong. Choose to do what is right.

God doesn't lead you into temptation, but sometimes he allows you to be tested.

Too often, you may see temptation as a one-time occurrence, but in reality, you need to be constantly on guard.

When facing temptation, use the word of God.

Temptation seems attractive when you are in a position of being wounded or hurt physically or emotionally.

Stop temptation before it's too strong or moving too fast too control.

Temptation starts with a thought and becomes sin, and when you reflect on that thought, you allow it to take action. Then it becomes like a snowball rolling downhill—it grows more destructive the more you let it have its way.

Wisdom

When you confront an issue that seems beyond your physical power, remember that others have also shared your experience.

Understanding when to run is of great significance in spiritual warfare, as well as knowing when and how to fight in battle.

Using your time wisely builds your faith walk found in God's word, and the truth builds up your life.

Learn from other people's mistakes.

Possessing wisdom is the key to understanding.

Facts or reality not tried or tested by life's experiences become uninteresting.

Don't give a personal guarantee on a person's credit. Be sure you know that person well, and even then, if you're not sure, it's better to say nothing than to suffer later.

To gain understanding, you must be instructed.

Make sure that when you reach out to others, your own footing is safe and secure.

The Bible is full of medicine that works only when you apply it to the areas that are affected.

About the Author

Arletha Simpson is a teacher, mother, and now author of her first book. Through prayer, reading, and mediation on the word of God, she was inspired to write this book of aphorisms.

Arletha was born in Waycross, Georgia. She was raised in the church and accepted Christ as her Lord and Savior at an early age. She attended Ware County High School and then went on to teach as an assistant in a middle school in her hometown. She has been trained to help others through the word of God. She now resides in Atlanta, Georgia.

Printed in the United States
By Bookmasters